Giggle Factor
A Grownup Fairy Tale

Esther Hart

Published by Heart Solutions

Library and Archives Canada Cataloguing in Publication

Hart, Esther, [date].
Giggle factor : a grownup fairy tale / Esther Hart.

ISBN 978-0-9683364-4-1

1. Self-realization. 2. Self-actualization (Psychology). I. Title.

BF637.S4H355 2011   158.1   C2011-904193-6

Giggle factor … A theory of science which appears too ridiculous to be seriously considered is said to have a "high giggle factor."

Mr. Edison, you won't get past the giggle factor. No one believes you can make a machine talk!

From Urban Dictionary

Dedication

To all the people who have shared their
ideas and philosophies with the world so
that I might be guided to my inner truth.

Acknowledgements

Everyone who has come into my life has blessed me in their own special way. My friends and family love and support me no matter how "Aquarian" I get.

Some people contributed especially in the writing of Giggle *Factor*.

June Swadron listened to me as I explored my philosophies and asked just the right questions to help me bring them into focus. She assured me that when the time was right, the book would be written effortlessly. She was right. She also provided insightful edits to the first draft.

Caroline Lennox listened to me share the theme of the book with such enthusiasm, one day over tea, that I was inspired to write what had been percolating for a year and a half. Then she added her brilliant editing ideas.

No one matches Rebecca Kennel when it comes to proofreading. She finds every missing or extra comma and every single grammatical error.

I thank all of you from the bottom of my heart.

Contents

Dedication i

Acknowledgements iii

Prologue 1

1 Terror 5

2 Evolution 11

3 Control 15

4 There Are No Mistakes 25

5 Getting Out of the Pit 33

6 More Revelations 37

7 Let Yourself off the Hook 43

8 I Need Do Nothing 45

9 Money, Money, Money 49

10 The Giggle Factor 55

Prologue

Once upon a time ... oooops ... that's not quite right. Where I am there is no time. There isn't even a where. Actually there aren't even words. Therefore I don't have a name, but, since you understand everything through words, you can call me Giggle.

I am the creator of words. With words I created stories. I created stories of the sun, moon, stars, planets and vast universes; stories of people, animals and plants; stories of science, religion and philosophy; stories of gods and goddesses. Everything you ever heard of is a story that I created with words.

I am such a great story teller that the stories appear real, certainly most of the characters in the stories think they are real—until they become aware of "The Giggle Factor" that is. After that the story changes quite dramatically.

Think of yourself as a character in a fiction novel. You have a relationship with the author but you can't know the author because you're not real. You seem real. Of course you do. Everything in your experience seems real. When you get hurt, it really hurts. When you touch something it feels solid. How can you imagine that a table or a person is not real?

You can't, because that's how I created the story of you.

Just like in a novel, where the characters appear to be making decisions, but obviously it's the author making all the decisions, you probably feel like you're making choices and you might even be feeling guilty about some of those choices. "Whoa," I can hear you screaming, "of course I make choices and my experience is the result of the choices I make. My thoughts create my reality."

Well, that's another story I created. But have you noticed that it's not reliable?

Sometimes you have positive thoughts and something positive happens and you think, "Look what I created with my thoughts." Other times you have positive thoughts and your life seems to go "down the drain." Then you think, "I did something wrong. I must be blocking what I really want." Then you beat yourself up and hunt and hunt for what you're blocking.

You can let all that go now. You can rest in the assurance that everything that ever happened in the story of your life was created by me, Giggle. You have never done anything wrong and you never will. You don't make mistakes and you are never bad or wrong. You are never "not enough" or "not good enough." You are the exact perfect story that I created: a story of love and hate, joy and sadness, peace and war, comfort and pain, beauty and ugliness, good and bad.

You may have heard the saying that FEAR means False Evidence Appearing Real. Actually all Evidence is False, even though it convinces you that you or your experiences are Real. There is nothing real and nothing to fear. Your story will unfold exactly the way I create it. You will never be punished for your choices. You will only have experiences. Some you will like and some you won't. It's how I wrote your story.

You can let go of judging people who don't agree with you or behave in ways you don't approve of. They are not wrong and neither are you.

You have your own unique story. Whether you believe in a religious teaching, astrology, psychic phenomenon, extra terrestrials or any other belief system, your story is true—for you. Every story I ever created is true—*and it's not real.*

Giggle

1 Terror

Star felt the terror and it confused her. She wasn't used to feeling this intense fear and hopelessness. She couldn't recognize the thoughts as her thoughts. It felt as if something or someone had invaded her body and taken over her mind.

She was used to knowing that there was a solution to everything. She could remember when she was in her thirties and had become the manager of a symphony orchestra with her only training for the job being a year and a half as the administrative assistant. She had excelled in that position. She had an inner knowing that whatever she needed would show up for her.

In fact, one morning on her way to work she heard a giggle in the back of her head and then the thought, "You don't have to know how, you just have to be willing." Many times she experienced thoughts coming to her, guiding her to where she needed to be and what she needed to do even though there was nothing in her past experience that would have prepared her to know those things.

Now, 20 years later, she had lost all of that knowing. She was aware of the loss and had no idea how to get it back.

She didn't even know what had caused the terror.

For many years she had been on a conscious journey of discovery. She had even written a book that had inspired many people. Her counsel was sought by people in distress. By sharing insights that she had gained, she was able to assist those people to find peace in their lives.

She had come through several occasions when money had become scarce and had trusted that all was as it should be and that all would be well. She experienced times of fear and loss of control, but they never lasted very long and there was always a sense that something would work out.

Just before the terror hit, Star was soaring. She was living and working at a retreat centre where she had the opportunity to share her insights with many people. That is what she thrived on, seeing people's lives change by embracing new ways of seeing things.

She had just been introduced to a new business opportunity that she could incorporate into what she was already doing and that also made a difference in people's lives. Star spent the last of her savings to get involved and had the confidence that she was being guided into this new way of life.

She was ecstatic. She was sure that once again her life was in a wonderful flow.

The next moment she felt paralysed, like the wind had been kicked out of her stomach. Suddenly her focus became the fact that she no longer had a nest egg of cash to create a sense of security. She was surprised. Her cash flow had been tighter than this before and it hadn't caused this devastation.

Yet, even though she had a place to live, food to eat and people who promised that she would be taken care of, she could only feel the despair. The reality of her safety could not penetrate her thinking. She was sure she would not survive. There was nothing logical in the fear. It was just there. Her ability to know that there was a solution to every situation had vanished.

The thought came to her, "Star, you know that you are a storyteller. You know that you inspire people by sharing your stories. This is just another story that you will share."

Star screamed back, "Are you nuts? Do you think I'm going to share this shameful story with anyone? How could my feeling hopeless and useless and wanting to die be inspiring to anyone? Besides, I have to survive to tell the story and there is no way I can survive this."

Yet she kept hearing the thought, "Trust yourself. Trust yourself. Trust yourself."

Day after day Star did her work effectively. Yet it didn't register in her mind that she was just as competent as before. The fear was always there, nagging. She was constantly looking for something to do that would make her feel productive and at least a little worthwhile. When she went back to her room at the end of the day, she would curl up in her bed and cry, hoping not to wake up in the morning and have to face the terror again. Yet each day it was there.

One day she was watching a movie and saw people golfing. Star thought, "I like to golf." The thought came as a shock. It was the first time in a long time that she had a sense of desire. She had become numb, sure that she had no future. Now a glimmer of light shone into her darkness.

After three months of heavy darkness, the curtain began to lift. Gradually, more and more light came in and a sense of possibility returned.

2 Evolution

When Star left home at 19 she was aware that she could not follow what she considered the radical evangelical teachings of her father. She abhorred his hypocrisy, preaching about God's love and forgiveness, yet living in fear and threatening violence to the family. She had a sense that she needed to find something that worked for her, something that was possible to live up to.

She didn't go searching, just lived her life, carrying with her much of the fear and guilt that had been well embedded in her being.

11

The guilt was magnified by the fact that she became pregnant while still single. She had agonized over what to do. She would have loved to be able to keep her child but could not imagine raising a child with a grandfather that considered "illegitimate" children an abomination. She did what she felt was best for the child—disappeared to a big city to have her child in secret and give her up for adoption.

She subsequently married and had another child, Millicent.

When Millicent was born the thought came to Star, "Every mistake I ever made was because of lack of self-confidence. I will raise this child to make all her decisions based on what she feels is right for her, no matter what anyone else thinks, including me." This was a tough challenge for someone raised in a disciplinarian household, yet Star embraced this intention. Millicent became a teacher for Star, showing her what it was like to be natural, rather than swayed by other people's opinions and expectations.

In her thirties, Star began to read books that gave her different insights into spiritual ideas. She began to accept that there were other options than the Christian belief of heaven for believers and hell for nonbelievers. Yet, even as she embraced this new-found freedom, when she watched television evangelists speaking about hell-fire, she had to leave the room before the vortex of fear sucked her back in.

Over time, this fear also subsided and Star felt free to believe whatever she chose without concern for eternal damnation.

Star began to read voraciously. She read in one of Wayne Dyer's books that we are spiritual beings having a human experience, and it resonated with her. She also liked his suggestion that if we live by the words of a children's song, we could be at peace. The song goes:

Row, row, row your boat, gently down the stream. Merrily, merrily, merrily, merrily, life is but a dream.

Star attended a talk by Dr. Norman Vincent Peale and was moved by his low-key presentation on his theory of the power of positive thinking. She read books that suggested that you could be happy all the time, you just had to choose it. She liked that one. She wanted to be happy. When a friend asked her if she ever cried. Her response was, "Why would I want to cry. I want to be happy? If I think of something that might make me cry, I just think a happy thought."

When she was asked how she was, Star's response was often, "I would tell you that it couldn't get better, but it always does." She loved her career. She loved her family. She loved her life. She felt like she was living a fairy tale. And it was a fairy tale—she just didn't realize it at the time.

It was when she was in her mid-forties that the bubble burst, and the evolution of her awareness became intentional.

3 Control

As Star reflected on her life, she realized that control had always been important to her. For example, she never wanted to get drunk because she would be out of control. She couldn't pinpoint what she thought would happen if she were out of control, she just knew that it wasn't an acceptable state for her.

She suspected it came down to fear. Fear was the most predominant emotion she remembered from her childhood. She was afraid of making her father angry. She was afraid that the communists were coming to torture and kill them. She was afraid that she would die in sin and go to hell. Later she was afraid of her father's threats to kill the whole family and then himself. She was determined to be a very good little girl which, from what she knows now about the rebel side of her, required a great deal of control. What made it easier was her abhorrence of conflict. She always wanted to keep peace. As a young child, a scolding for asking permission to do the "wrong" thing affected her so deeply that it was enough to keep her from intentionally doing anything to arouse her father's anger.

As Star reached her early teens, her older sister, Samantha, was dating. One evening Samantha was out late and their father became very angry. Samantha and Star shared a room, and, after Samantha came to bed, their father came in and held a knife to her throat and threatened her. This strongly reinforced Star's determination to be a very good girl. It also caused her to feel a great deal of shame for pretending to be asleep and not having the courage to try to help her sister.

Star used to think that being in control of her emotions was something to be admired. It kept her from falling apart when she gave up her baby girl for adoption. It kept her from feeling the pain of that loss for the next 24 years. She was proud of the fact that if anyone, any time, anywhere asked her how she was, the answer was, "Terrific." And she meant it. One day when she was in a very high stress job, she responded with "Terrific" when a colleague asked her how she was. He asked, "How can you be terrific when you do the job you do?"

Her reply was, "Because I choose to be."

Then he asked, "Are you always terrific?"

She said, "No. I start every day that way. Most days it gets better."

When Star and Jonathan were transferred to another city, things continued to fall into place for Star. Even though everyone said there were no jobs, Star had one secured before she even moved there. What a high that was. She had been reading the material that said we create our experiences. She felt in control of her life and with that control came a sense of security.

She soon found out that control and security are illusions. That job ended. For nine months she found nothing. She went to see Angelica, a psychic, who taught Star to give herself permission to be out of work. She said Star needed to be free to work on her inner healing. What a concept—to put all her energy into her own well-being. She told Star that, when it was time for her to work, a job would show up. Star said, "So I shouldn't be beating myself up over the fact that I'm not pounding the pavement eight hours a day looking for work?"

Angelica replied, "Absolutely not." She assured Star that in fact she was bringing into her life exactly what she needed. She also told her that she needed to feel safe. Star hadn't realized that she didn't feel safe, but, of course, why would she have the desperate need to be in control if she felt safe. The psychic worked through an exercise with her that had her imagine herself filled with, and surrounded by, the light of unconditional love. That helped but it wasn't a complete cure.

Star sensed that her parents did the best they could. Unfortunately, they used fear as a tool. Now, as an adult, in order to feel safe, Star had to unlearn the fears that her parents taught her in an effort to keep her safe. Star wished her parents had raised her with confidence instead of fear.

One day, when Star thought she had found the perfect job with a divorce support group, she arrived home to be greeted by her husband, Jonathan, with the information that they needed to talk. Star was pleased. There had been a great deal of tension between them, and she was glad that they would have a discussion and resolve the tension. Millicent had grown up and left home and it was time to take advantage of the freedom and create some romance. Jonathan had come to the same conclusion about having romance; however, he had become convinced that it was not possible between the two of them and that the marriage was over.

When Star was honest with herself, she had to agree that this was a wise decision. Despite the fact that she had liked, admired and even loved Jonathan, she did not have strong romantic feelings for him. After getting over her anger about the fact that he had taken the control away from her, making the decision without discussing it first, Star began to see the gift that he had given her.

Jonathan had taken on the agonizing task of coming to the conclusion that they both needed to be free. He fretted over how to tell Star, knowing that he was going to hurt her. By offering her a *fait accompli* he saved Star from once again trying to bend herself into a pretzel to try to please him. With the help of a kind friend, Michael, she very quickly saw that she had been offered the gift of freedom to explore more possibilities in her life. She embraced the opportunity wholeheartedly.

Star began to soar. She was elated. She moved into a fabulous condo with an incredible view of the ocean. She finally found a job, and she loved it. It entertained her. She had friends and family that she loved and that loved her. On the surface her life looked very desirable.

Yet she fluctuated between ecstasy and desperation? She did not want to wake up in the morning and have to face making decisions about her life? She felt pressured to be doing something meaningful. She knew that she had many of skills that she was not putting to use.

Star had moments when she felt out of control. The best way she could describe it was to say that she felt as if she needed to leave her body. When it happened at her desk at work, she would close her eyes and say, "OK go." During breaks at work she played a computer game called "Taipei", because, if she won, there was a fortune cookie-type message on the screen that would say something positive about the future. She needed that reinforcement to get her through the day. At first the feeling of needing to leave her body happened two weeks apart. Then it was once a week. When it happened twice in one week, she imagined that it could become permanent and she would be completely insane.

One day Star found herself on the floor kicking and screaming. She was horrified. She was not used to getting highly emotional. She was used to being calm and accepting. She phoned Michael to say that she thought she was going insane. His reply was, "Congratulations. Now you know you're not in control. The only way to go is up."

When Star mentioned this conversation to Michael later, he said, "That's awful. Did I really say that?"

Star's reply was, "Yes, and it's the best thing you could have said."

Some time later when reading something by Carolyn Myss, Star learned that in early times the monks understood that in order to gain awareness, the feeling of insanity was a given. She cheered, "Yeah. It's not just me."

In the meantime, Star was feeling out of control because she couldn't see her future. While she had been out of work for nine months she had lost her faith in herself. The self-help books said, and she agreed, that if you believe, you can create what you want. Her previous experience had been that wonderful things showed up in her life, often even before she knew she wanted them. She had never really had to go after anything. Now she had all this freedom and the opportunity to do whatever she wanted, and she couldn't remember what her deepest dreams and desires were. People and books would advise, "Find your passion and everything will fall into place." She wanted to scream and tear out her hair. She wanted someone to tell her what her passion was and put her out of her agony.

Letting go of control and feeling safe and loved was a challenging journey for Star. That, combined with not knowing what she was supposed to be doing, had her on verge of collapse. In addition to feeling like she wanted to leave her body, she also did not want to wake up in the morning. She wanted to be free of the heavy responsibility of finding her purpose and making the most of her life. She wasn't satisfied just to live each day. She felt obligated to live up to her potential and be the most that she could be.

Fortunately, she believed Michael when he said she could only get better. One day she started thinking about what "being in control" had really looked like. She realized that all she had apparently controlled was her emotions. In doing so, she had denied herself the gift of experiencing pain. She asked herself, "If my thoughts were given control of a part of my body, what part would continue to function? Would I like to have control of my blinking? Certainly not. What about my heart or lungs? Definitely not. What about one tiny skin cell?" It became very clear that not a single cell of her body would continue to function if she were in control. Then she thought, "If I can't control even the minutest part of my body, whatever made me think that I could control my whole being within the vastness of the universe?" At that moment she decided to give up the need to be in control. She realized that, as a conscientious person, she had always done a good job of what she was given to do. So she started each day with this meditation, "I'm here. I'm willing. Show me."

As a child in Sunday school and church she always heard about surrender to God, but her impression at that time was that it meant sacrificing all the fun things in life. Now, surrender meant giving up the need to be in control, accepting that her life is already in tune with God, living each day as an experience and knowing that she was not alone.

Best of all, she had learned the gift of feeling pain. She began crying often. Sometimes she knew what triggered it and sometimes she didn't. But the tears felt like a celebration of life. She had been given the opportunity to feel and because she could feel the pain, her joy was far more bountiful.

4 There Are No Mistakes

For 23 years after walking out of the hospital without her beautiful baby, Treena, Star told no one. She kept this secret to herself because she felt so much shame. She thought that she would keep the secret for the rest of her life. When she signed the adoption papers she was told that they would be sealed forever.

Then she started hearing stories about people being reunited with children they had given up for adoption. She considered the possibility for herself. She was willing to make the contact but agonized that it might not be in Treena's best interests. Star eventually decided to go ahead.

Her next hurdle was to tell Millicent. Her relationship with Millicent had always been exceptional, and she was afraid that this information would make Millicent lose respect for her.

After all those years of not speaking about Treena, it was very difficult to get the words out. Eventually, Star said to Millicent, "Before I met your father, I had a baby girl that I gave up for adoption and I want to find her."

Millicent's immediate response was, "Oh, Mom, I'm so proud of you."

Star burst into tears. How could someone be proud of her for something that had caused her so much shame? Millicent hugged her mom and whispered, "When can I meet my sister?" A little later Millicent approached Star with a concerned look on her face.

Star asked, "Honey, what's wrong?"

Millicent replied, "I'm just so sad that I got to grow up with you and she didn't."

Again Star was brought to tears. This time they were tears of gratitude for having such a generous child.

Star's next step was to call Social Services because the baby had been adopted through their agency. They referred her to the Adoption Reunion Registry. The Registry gave her two options. The Passive Search was a matter of connecting two people who had both registered. The Active Search consisted of the agency finding the other party and notifying them that they were being sought. Star immediately applied for the Passive Search. After that, every trip to the mailbox was filled with anticipation. Then the letter arrived. There was no match, but if she chose she could do the active search.

Once again she agonized. Treena was now an adult and surely if she wanted to be found she would have put herself on the list. On the other hand, what if she felt rejected and was afraid of being rejected again?

During this time Star was still married. Then her marriage ended and she decided that now was the time to find her daughter no matter what the circumstances. She wanted Treena to know that she was available to her in case knowing Star could benefit her and Star wanted to know what Treena's life was like. Star would let her know that she would not interfere in any way with her family or her life. She wanted so much for Treena to know that she had not been abandoned or rejected, that her being given up for adoption was not because Star didn't want her.

Again the trips to the mailbox made Star's heart race with expectancy. Within two weeks, a letter arrived from Claire, the person in charge of the search, saying that they had found Treena and would be sending a letter to notify her that they had information of importance to her.

Again Star waited.

One day at noon Star felt an urgency to check for phone messages because she was sure that Claire had called. She was right. When she called back, Claire's first words were, "I'm so glad you called before Treena got here to sign the papers."

What a lot of information those few words provided. Her name was Treena; she had received the letter and was willing to be contacted. Then Claire told Star that Treena had a 9-month-old baby girl.

"WOW! I'm a grandmother."

It was arranged that Treena would call Star that evening. She was excited and elated. She yelled as loud as she could.

She phoned Millicent and said, "You have a niece."

And then Millicent started screaming.

Star and Treena had a long, friendly conversation and arranged to meet for lunch. As Star watched her approach, she could immediately see a family resemblance. Star kept looking at Treena and thinking, "This lovely young woman is the baby I gave away."

It felt like a dream instead of reality.

Treena's adoptive mom, Carolyn, had invited Star to their home to have dinner with the rest of the immediate family. Star had decided not to take gifts because she didn't want anyone to think that she was trying to buy affection. Instead she took a plant and a card.

In the card she wrote, "Thank you so much for giving Treena a home when I couldn't. Thank you even more for sharing her with me now. Please be assured that I don't want to be the cause of anyone's pain. I just want Treena to know that I'm here for her if she needs me." Carolyn showed Star pictures of Treena throughout her life and the two mothers spent the day thanking each other. Carolyn also gave Star the following poem:

Legacy of an Adopted Child
Author unknown
Once there were two women
Who never knew each other.
One you do not remember,
The other you call mother.
Two different lives
Shaped to make yours one.
One became your guiding star,
The other became your sun.
The first gave you life
And the second taught you to live in it.
The first gave you a need for love
And the second was there to give it.
One gave you a nationality,
The other gave you a name.
One gave you the seed of talent,
The other gave you aim.

One gave you emotions,
The other calmed your fears.
One saw your first sweet smile
The other dried your tears.
One gave you up -
It was all that she could do.
The other prayed for a child
And god led her straight to you.
And now you ask me
Through your tears,
The age-old Question
Throughout the years:
Heredity or environment -
Which are you the product of?
Neither, my darling, neither,
Just two different kinds of love.

A short time later, Millicent and Treena met. The girls fell in love with each other at first sight. In the evening, Star and her two daughters were sitting in the kitchen. As Star looked at these two girls, one that she considered a mistake and the other that she thought of as an accident, she thought, "Thank God for stupid mistakes."

The next thought that came shocked her. It was, "Star, there are no mistakes."

Star began to wonder. What if that were true? It was hard to fathom. She wasn't sure she could accept that. Then she thought, "Even if it's not true, what if I lived as if it were true? Would it change how I experience my life?" She began to experiment and sure enough, when she remembered, her life felt better.

When she forgot, life could get very hard. It was so easy for her to feel that she wasn't doing enough. She knew she had been given a good mind, great health and many talents. She kept thinking that there was more that she should be doing. It caused her to be unable to appreciate the great things she had in her life.

Then one day she had the thought, "All that is required of me is to do what feels right to do with what shows up to do because I am one with the Source." In that moment she was at peace, believing that whatever she did was enough.

And then she forgot, again.

5 Getting Out of the Pit

Once Star had seen a glimmer of light, hope returned. It was amazing the difference a little hope made.

It felt as if whatever had taken over her mind had left. However, she felt bruised. She had to learn to live in the light all over again.

She started to question her beliefs about our thoughts creating our reality. Hadn't she been in an incredibly positive state the moment before she landed in the pit? And how could the thoughts of despair while in the pit have resulted in getting her that glimmer of light?

Was there something else going on? And if so, what was it?

The last time she had been in despair, she had gotten out by challenging her beliefs. She had gained insights that brought her peace and yet she wasn't living by those insights. She had been listening to other people's beliefs that conflicted with hers.

Star had accepted the notion that it is our innate right to be wealthy and healthy, and if we're not, we are doing something wrong. We need to be diligently working at "fixing" ourselves so we can live our "full potential". This all fed into her shame and guilt around not being enough or doing enough.

One day a colleague said something that Star took as a put down. She felt herself begin the spiral into the pit of self-loathing. Suddenly the thought came to her, "Nothing she can think or say about you can diminish your value." Star sat up a little straighter and began to feel better.

Immediately another thought came. "Star, nothing you can think, say or do can diminish your value." She sat up even straighter.

Then she heard, "Star, nothing you can think, do or say can increase your value. Your value is eternal." This put a smile on her face and again she felt peace.

Then she forgot again.

6 More Revelations

Star was healing but still struggling. She woke up every morning with a sense of dread. Could she do "enough" today? Her financial needs were being met, she had a lovely home and people who loved her. Yet she felt that something was wrong with her that prevented her from creating wealth. She surely had the skills to generate wealth. She often heard the phrase, "What's blocking you?" She felt pressured to find out what it was and fix it. It was a chore to get out of bed and "get at it" and that led to guilt.

Then she read a book called *Busting Loose from the Money Game* by Robert Scheinfeld. The book supported what she had known and had been afraid to trust. Some of the philosophies expressed in the book were that we are not real; everything on the planet is like a hologram that appears real but isn't. The hologram has no authority to change itself. The hologram is the result of energy projected onto a field of possibilities and it is from that place that change occurs. What works for a person once, may not work the second time. What works for one person may not work for another.

By combining her sense of knowing with the philosophies in the book, Star came to the following conclusions:

- There is no reliable "cause and effect" relationship on the planet.
- The notion that, "If I do what you did, I'll get what you got," is not reliable.
- Everyone has their own perfect journey and it may look good—or not. I am not a failure if I don't achieve wealth or if I become ill. It is simply my story.

- I am not in control of anything, not even my thoughts.
- Having money does not solve money issues—many people with a great deal of money are still afraid they don't have enough.

Even though Star felt encouraged to trust her inner knowing, the fear did not immediately diminish. The book offered a process to help move into a different phase of experience. Star wanted to believe that her life could change, but she was afraid that even if she did the process, once again, nothing would change. She was encouraged that Robert didn't promise that she would experience the same outcome he had. She did the process.

It was not her desire to change her outer circumstances but to be at peace no matter what the outer circumstances were. She no longer defined freedom as having financial "security." Freedom was: being free of financial concerns no matter what her bank account looked like. Accepting that the script would be what it would be. That her life would unfold as it would without her "making it happen." That if her bank account was low it wasn't because she was stupid or lazy or not willing to "do what it takes." Not even a depleted bank account could diminish her value.

Much to her surprise, her life did begin to change. Once again, she practiced living as if her knowings were actually true. She embraced that everything on this planet is a hologram and not actually real. That's what the physicists are saying anyway. She imagined life here as being like a movie. No matter how much she didn't like a scene in a movie, every time she played it the same thing happened. The only way to change what she saw on the screen was to play a different movie. The film maker had to make a different film to project onto the screen. The characters on the screen could not change anything. Since she saw herself as a character on the screen, she was not responsible for the role she was playing in the movie.

Star used this philosophy as a self-forgiveness tool. When she did something that she felt bad about, she would remind herself that she was living her script perfectly and that she couldn't have done it differently. That didn't stop her from apologizing for the behaviour.

Gradually, over time, it took less reminding and became natural to live as if the script was perfect and that Star could trust that she had never made, would never make and, in fact, couldn't make a mistake. Her financial "security" came from knowing that whatever she was experiencing was the perfect experience. Even if what happened wasn't fun, it was much better than living what looked like the perfect life on the outside while experiencing guilt, shame and dread on the inside.

7 Let Yourself off the Hook

Star was doing a business that she had thought was her vehicle for creating financial freedom. It was a good business, and she derived great satisfaction from being able to assist people in creating more vibrant health for themselves. Yet, she had not achieved the financial success that she anticipated.

For a long time she blamed herself, thinking that she was doing something wrong. It triggered her underlying belief that she could never be enough or do enough.

One day she was advised that her leadership was no longer needed. At first she felt angry and betrayed and then the thought came to her that this new situation afforded her a great deal of freedom. She celebrated.

Some time later she shared this story with a colleague who said, "So you've let yourself off the hook." For a few seconds, Star felt beginnings of the dreaded sense of not being enough. Then she heard a giggle in the back of her head and felt a smile come to her lips. The next thought was, "Star, over the last few months you have felt more freedom, happiness and joy than you have for many years. It's not because your physical situation has changed. It is, in fact, precisely because you have let yourself off the hook."

She then had a vision of a wall with coat hooks and people hanging on the hooks flailing. She saw clearly that she had expended a lot of energy getting nowhere because she had herself on the hook of thinking she should do certain things in order to achieve certain outcomes that other people had suggested she should achieve.

8 I Need Do Nothing

Waking thoughts were a good indicator of Star's level of peace in her life. For a long time, when she went to bed at night, she would plan on how late she could stay in bed the next morning. Some mornings she would decide to stay in bed even longer and then would feel guilty. One morning, when she had given herself permission to stay in bed an extra hour, she suddenly found herself responding to an idea and jumping out of bed after just a few minutes. She realized that instead of enjoying the time in bed, she had spent it feeling guilty.

During that time some friends of Star's were studying a book called *The Way of Mastery*. Star got a powerful insight from just one page in the book. On that page was the phrase "I need do nothing." A question was posed about the need to survive. The response indicated that we don't actually need to survive.

Star's response was a fist flung in the air with, "YES! It didn't say, 'I will do nothing,' it said, 'I need do nothing.' If I need do nothing then I can watch and see what, in fact, I do."

Star decided that she would experiment with relaxing, enjoying lying in bed and watching to see what would inspire her to get up.

One day Star woke up and realized that she had no dread. She watched to see how her life would unfold.

Star became more and more peaceful with her life. She was almost completely free of her "saint complex" — the feeling that she needed to be perfect, always good, caring, loving and liked by everyone. One day she received a phone call with some information that made her very angry. She hung up the phone and started ranting in her head about how furious she was. Then she started laughing about how good it felt to be furious and not think that she was too "spiritual" to get angry. With her laughter came the thought, "I bet I'll find out that I completely misunderstood, and there was nothing to be mad about." That is exactly what happened. She still felt good about being able to enjoy feeling furious.

Over time a notion solidified in Star's mind. The notion was this. "I am a character in a fiction novel and I am not the author. I have no more authority over my experience than a character in a novel. My life can change at a moment's notice and make no sense whatsoever because a fiction writer doesn't have to follow any rules of nature."

It made perfect sense. It explained why so often things happen in people's lives that seem completely unbelievable. As she saw her life like a novel, she would imagine that each night she was finishing a page with no idea what would be on the next page the following day. It might follow logically, or it might go in a completely different direction.

The more Star looked at it, the more she saw that every aspect of her life made sense from this perspective. She was also profoundly relieved that after all her years of not measuring up, she had finally found a philosophy that she could live up to—no more hypocrisy.

9 Money, Money, Money

You may have guessed that, like many people, Star's experience was greatly affected by money. She grew up thinking her family was poor and when she was 15 years old she decided that her philosophy for happiness was, "Want what you have or what is in your power to achieve."

Throughout her marriage, there were times when money was a little tight, yet there was always enough for a lovely home, clothes and vacations. She always had a job when she wanted one. Star didn't consider herself ambitious. All she wanted was a "nice" life.

Then the time came when she wanted a job and couldn't get one. This was when she began to have feelings of worthlessness. For nine months she searched for that illusive "reliable" income. Each Monday she would pray, "What miracle will we create this week?" She did not know from week to week where the money would come from to pay her bills. Yet every month her bills got paid. Sometime she would get small surprise contracts. Sometimes she had to resort to asking family and friends for loans. This was very hard for her. She felt ashamed and stupid for having gotten herself into this situation.

During this time, she did not fall into despair. Somehow she was able to live in trust. This was actually a surprise to Star. She had often read of people who live day to day trusting that their needs would be met. She had been sure that she would not be able to do that. At least, she would surely never make a conscious decision to live that way.

Then one day Star met Carol. Carol was impressed with Star and her talents and invited Star to come and work with her. Star was ecstatic. Finally the drought had ended and she would once again have a steady cash flow. As conversations about the work involved continued, Star began to feel uneasy. The uneasiness turned into severe discomfort. Finally Star realized that this was not a good fit. It wasn't fair to Carol and it wasn't fair to her to take this position.

She called Carol and told her. When Star got off the phone she shouted, "YES!" She was thrilled with herself for having the courage to make that call and continue to live in trust.

Then she shouted, "Okay. I've given up this job that isn't right for me, now you have to get me something else!"

Within 10 days she had a call from another friend offering her a sweet opportunity.

It took months for Star to adjust to feeling the safety of a "reliable" income. A year later that job was gone. Star had saved diligently so she had a bit of a cushion. As that depleted, she was once again wondering where the money would come from. She would gladly have taken a "regular" job but that didn't seem to be her path.

As she lived from month to month she came to some

realizations about her belief about money.

One was, "I have to control the money so I don't starve. I have to be in control to survive." The next thought that came to her mind was. "I surrender. I have never been in control. I let go of being tight-fisted. I open to the flow."

Another realization was, "I have never suffered physically from lack of money. I have suffered tremendously from my thoughts about lack of money."

One day Star realized that money is the easiest problem in the world to solve because someone can give you money.

They can't just hand over health, a good relationship or peace of mind, but they can give you money. In that moment she decided, "If all I have to worry about is money, I have nothing to worry about." She called on this statement often when the temptation to worry came to mind.

Star was aware that her sense of security was tied to money. It was tempting to believe that when there is money in the bank there is security. Then she realized that bank accounts—and especially investments—don't provide security. They can be gone in an instant. In order to feel safe she developed the philosophy that "the only real security is trust."

Some of Star's suffering around money came from believing what other people said such as:

- Wealth is our spiritual birthright and, if you're not wealthy, you're not living up to your potential
- If you will do the work to remove your blocks, you too can be wealthy
- You should want to be wealthy and to do whatever it takes

These beliefs about money began to dissolve when she read Busting Loose from the Money Game. As she accepted that her life was a script that had already been written, that she would have all the money she needed to live the script, she was able to stop berating herself for finding herself in a less than favourable financial position.

Star began to relish the experience of trusting every moment that her life was perfect—that even the occasional worry about money was perfect. It was her experience and she was going to experience it fully. She remembered how much she had admired people, in stories she had heard, who lived day to day with what showed up for them. She also saw how frightened people were who appeared to have financial security that they didn't trust.

For a short time Star was once again offered "reliable" income. She enjoyed it. Then that ended and she felt an inner excitement for the next adventure in her life. There was no fear or worry. No affirmations were necessary. She was at peace. She had embodied the assurance, that she had known in her mind, that her life was unfolding perfectly.

She had become so peaceful and happy that one day a friend said to her, "Star, I want to live the way you do."

Star replied, "I'm not sure that's true. I think what you want is to be as happy as I am."

10 The Giggle Factor

Star's friends saw that she was happier than she had ever been. Even though she had very little money, her life was abundant.

One day Star shared with Jennifer her philosophy of having no authority over her life. Jennifer's response was, "Of course I create my experiences. I create them with my thoughts. When I have positive thoughts I feel happy and when I have negative thoughts I feel miserable."

Star asked, "Where do the thoughts come from?"

Jennifer replied, "I choose them."

Star asked, "Can you choose any thought you want any time you want? I read in *Zero Limits* by Joe Vitale that scientists claim they have evidence that decisions are made before they reach the level of consciousness."

Jennifer quipped, "Of course. I have free choice. I'm always able to choose."

"Then why would you ever choose negative thoughts if you prefer to feel happy and you can choose any thought you want? Don't you ever feel like what you're thinking is beyond your control?" Star enquired.

"Yes. I often feel that my thoughts are out of control, but I believe that my higher consciousness is creating the experience for me and the I that is really me is in control even though my conscious mind isn't necessarily in control."

Star smiled. "If that works for you, then it's definitely true for you, and I support you."

Star shared her philosophy whenever she was asked about it and as soon as she would notice that her friends couldn't quite grasp the concept for themselves, or were feeling defensive, she would change the subject. She had come to realize that everyone's story is true for them and it benefits no one to suggest that they are wrong. She only shared her idea in case it would resonate with people who were looking for just this information.

Star found that, with this philosophy, she could accept everyone exactly where they are. There had been a time when she condemned people for their beliefs and thought that some beliefs were more "advanced" than others. She came to realize that her "new-age" beliefs, with which she had replaced her Christian beliefs, were just as guilt inducing. The only difference was that with Christianity she blamed God and with the new-age philosophy she blamed herself. Now there was no one to blame, nothing to be blamed for, just an opportunity to have an experience.

One day, when Star was telling Jennifer how happy and free she was since she had started to live as if she was a character in a fiction novel, Jennifer asked Star, "What's the author's name?"

"Giggle."

"Giggle?"

"Yes, Giggle. I remember times in my life when I had a fearful thought and then I would notice a giggle in the back of my head and a thought would come that would drive the fear out. Here is a fun example. I was riding my bike on a busy road without a bike lane. The thought came to me that if I lost concentration for a few seconds, or if one of the drivers swerved just slightly, I could be killed. At that moment I heard the giggle and this thought, 'No need to think about that. You've got a lot to do here yet.' I continued bicycling along, smiling."

Often, when Star experienced what she considered a profound truth, the thought came to her with a giggle. So what better name to give the author of her life?

She doesn't expect her fairy tale to be "happily ever after." She doesn't expect to be an evolved spiritual being. She expects to have a fascinating human experience with its ups and downs.

When Star has moments of distress, they don't last long because she remembers the "Giggle Factor" and a smile comes to her face.

For more on the Giggle Factor go to:

www.estherhart.com

giggglefactor@gmail.com